Lift Him Up

John 12:32

Biblical Preaching 101

by Charles Thompson

"Preach the word; be prepared in season and out of season;
correct, rebuke and encourage—
with great patience and careful instruction."
(2 Timothy 4:2)

PURELILLY PRESS

ISBN: 978-1-965050-07-1

Published by Purelilly Press Publishing
Huntsville, Texas

First Printing, 2026

This book is dedicated to Dr. Gene Brown who taught me so much about ministry at Southwestern Assemblies of God University.

TABLE OF CONTENTS

INTRODUCTION

Are you called by God to preach? Preaching is a journey of a lifetime instead of a mere event. God is the One who calls a preacher and continues to develop him or her. My journey started in June of 1992 when I surrendered to be a pastor at Pineywoods Baptist Encampment. I was then given the opportunity to preach!

The first time I preached shows that preaching is a journey. I read straight off my pages, finished in ten minutes, and sweat completely down! Although this didn't go well, it did not mean I was not called! It is a process. I had stuff to learn then, and I'm still learning to this day.

I wrote this workbook on Biblical Preaching to encourage you and provide you the spiritual and practical tools needed to help you develop your call. I am passing on the things God taught me personally and through other men and women of God. In the following pages, you will find practical ways of hearing God on what to preach, various ways to study, and how to create a sermon outline from various techniques.

I would love to hear from you how the workbook helped you. Share your testimony at cht4jesus@gmail.com.

Be bold, be courageous, be confident,
Charles

CHAPTER 1

Are You Called?

I remember the day! As a kid, my cousin and I went into the woods to play. Guess what we were going to play? Church! I pretended I was preaching, and she pretended she was a member of the church who was listening. It was all fun and games, but it really spoke of something deeper that God was doing in me. I came to know later He had called me to preach the Word of God! Are you called to preach? This is the starting place for this workbook for an important reason. Fish swim, birds fly, bees buzz, grasshoppers jump, lions roar, snakes crawl, dogs bark, and cats meow! They were made to do that. The person who is called to preach is made to do it!

"13 For you created my inmost being; you knit me together in my mother's womb. 14 I praise you because I am fearfully and wonderfully made; your works are wonderful, I know that full well. 15 My frame was not hidden from you when I was made in the secret place, when I was woven together in the depths of the earth. 16 Your eyes saw my unformed body; all the days ordained for me were written in your book before one of them came to be. 17 How precious to me are your thoughts, God! How vast is the sum of them." (Psalm 139:13-17)

1. What was written in God's book (v16)?

_____

_____

_____

_____

_____

"4 The word of the Lord came to me, saying, 5 "Before I formed you in the womb I knew you, before you were born I set you apart; I appointed you as a prophet to the nations." 6 "Alas, Sovereign Lord," I said, "I do not know how to speak; I am too young." 7 But the Lord said to me, "Do not say, 'I am too young.' You must go to everyone I send you to and say whatever I command you. 8 Do not be afraid of them, for I am with you and will rescue you," declares the Lord. 9 Then the Lord reached out his hand and touched my mouth and said to me, "I have put my words in your mouth. 10 See, today I appoint you over nations and kingdoms to uproot and tear down, to destroy and overthrow, to build and to plant." (Jeremiah 1:4-10)

2. What did God set apart Jeremiah to do (v5)?

_____

_____

_____

_____

_____

3. What was Jeremiah's first objection (v6)?

_____

_____

_____

_____

_____

4. What was God's response to Jeremiah's objection (v7-10)?

_____

_____

_____

_____

_____

"Here is a trustworthy saying: Whoever aspires to be an overseer desires a noble task." (1 Timothy 3:1)

5. What two action words are used to describe someone wanting to be an overseer?

    _____
    _____
    _____
    _____
    _____

"So Christ himself gave the apostles, the prophets, the evangelists, the pastors and teachers." (Ephesians 4:11)

6. Whom did Christ give?

    _____
    _____
    _____
    _____
    _____

Each one of these verses communicates what we need to know about the call to preach.

-   God ordered the days of the preacher in His book before they were ever born to be a preacher of the Word of God!

-   Before the preacher was born, God appointed him or her to preach the Word of God just as Jeremiah was called to be a prophet.

-   Being called to preach has nothing to do with whether we *feel* qualified or not, because God qualifies us like He qualified Jeremiah.

- In being a preacher, you will have an internal desire and aspiration to preach the Word of God placed in you from the Almighty Himself.

- Preaching is an ability given by God.

Are you called to preach? Answering this question must occur before trying to learn how to preach or actually preach the Word of God. You might ask, "Why?" You must obey God's will for your life. If God's will is for you to preach the Word of God, then He will move heaven and earth to make a way and anoint you to do it. If it is not God's will for you, then you will be a square peg trying to fit into a round hole or a round peg trying to fit into a square hole. It will not work. You will be frustrated if it is not God's will for you, but you will be fulfilled if it is His will. The call to preach goes hand in hand with the call to pastor. You cannot pastor if you cannot preach. You can preach and not be a pastor though.

How Do You Know You Are Called to Preach?

God will put the desire in you to preach! It is a desire that will not go away no matter what. *"For God's gifts and his call are irrevocable." (Romans 11:29)*

God will confirm it to you through others.

When you preach, you will find personal fulfillment in doing it and feel energized during and after. It is because you are being who God called you to be.

God will confirm it to you through others who do not know, or who may know, that God has called you to preach.

In concluding this chapter, I will share when I knew I was called to preach. I was attending Summer camp at Pineywoods Baptist Encampment in the month of June in 1992. Evangelist Don Babbin was speaking, and, all of a sudden, the Holy Spirit nudged me to go forward during the altar call to surrender to be a pastor. I walked forward and told a youth counselor. I wrote it in the back of my Bible for memories sake. Upon coming home from youth camp, I told the church I was attending that I was called to pastor and wanted to get involved. Members of the church began to come up to me and ask me if I wanted to be a pastor as they felt that was God's call on my life. The rest is history! I have been preaching since 1992!

Preaching is not something everyone knows how to do automatically, and you cannot compare yourself to others. The first time I was asked to preach on a Wednesday night, it was quite uneventful. I prepared on computer paper what I wanted to say and then read it out loud without looking at anyone in the pews. I finished in 10 minutes and sweat completely down. Despite that shaky start, I continued to take more opportunities to preach. I got better and better. So, if you know you are called, do not give up because you do not feel you did as well as the pastor at your church who has been preaching for years. Take every opportunity you get and do not be hard on yourself.

CHAPTER 2

First Things First

Have you ever heard the saying, "Do not put the cart before the ox?" The ox goes before the cart because it is meant to pull the cart. The cart doesn't pull the ox! This is similar to preaching. I'll let Scripture explain this.

"38 As Jesus and his disciples were on their way, he came to a village where a woman named Martha opened her home to him. 39 She had a sister called Mary, who sat at the Lord's feet listening to what he said. 40 But Martha was distracted by all the preparations that had to be made. She came to him and asked, "Lord, don't you care that my sister has left me to do the work by myself? Tell her to help me!" 41 "Martha, Martha," the Lord answered, "you are worried and upset about many things, 42 but few things are needed—or indeed only one. Mary has chosen what is better, and it will not be taken away from her." (Luke 10:38-42)

1. What was Mary doing (vs 38-39)?

_____

_____

_____

_____

_____

2. What was Martha doing (v 40)?

_____
_____
_____
_____
_____

3. What did Jesus say to Martha (vs 41-42)?

_____
_____
_____
_____
_____

Preaching is not an end in itself. There is something more than preaching! Jesus also explained it very well.

"Love the Lord your God with all your heart and with all your soul and with all your mind and with all your strength." (Mark 12:30)

Jesus is more important than preaching. You are to love Jesus with all your heart, soul, mind, and strength…more than preaching. You might think, that sounds crazy! It isn't. Jesus is the source of good preachers and good preaching.

Your sermon preparation is not a substitute for your personal devotional time with Jesus.

Taking daily time with Jesus in the Word and prayer is being a Mary instead of a Martha. Mary chose wisely, and you should too. Being a Martha is being too busy for time with Jesus and then preparing sermons without being connected to the source of all sermons. He is the power behind all sermons. You cannot give what you do not personally have. Jesus wants you, not your sermon. Jesus loves you, not your sermon. The best sermons come from the ones who are spending devotional time with Jesus.

With all this said, I want to provide some helpful devotional tools for you to develop your relationship with the Lord.

SOAP

*"...to make her holy, cleansing her by **<u>the washing with water through the word</u>**, and to present her to himself as a radiant church, without stain or wrinkle or any other blemish, but holy and blameless." (Ephesians 5:26-27)*

S.O.A.P. STANDS FOR SCRIPTURE, OBSERVATION, APPLICATION, AND PRAYER.

It is a method of Bible journaling developed by Pastor Wayne Cordeiro. It's a great way to get more out of reading your Bible and allows you to record your thoughts, emotions, and the revelation you receive from God's Word.[1]

Scripture

Read meditatively and thoughtfully through a portion of Scripture. Pick a verse or two that stood out to you and write it in your journal.

Observation

Now write some observations about the verse(s) or passage. What is this passage or verse saying? About God? About people? How is Christ revealed in this?

---

[1] https://www.nlifefellowship.org/soap/

Application

Now write a few sentences on how this passage applies to your life. Is there truth about God that you are to believe? A promise to receive? Is the Holy Spirit convicting you of something you need to do or stop doing in light of God's truth? What specific principles are you challenged to practice based on scripture, prayer, and reflection? Be doers of the word and not merely hearers. (James 1:22)

Prayer

Now write out a prayer to God in response to this scripture. This is a way to turn God's Word to you back to Him. Be honest and express your heart to Him. God always listens and He delights in your prayers. (Psalm 34:15, Proverbs 15:8)

Title: _____

S – cripture: What verse or passage stood out to you?

_____

_____

_____

_____

_____

O – bservation: What stood out to you about this verse or passage?

_____

_____

_____

_____

_____

_____

_____

_____

_____

_____
_____
_____
_____

A – pplication: How can you apply what you learned from the verse or passage to your life?

_____
_____
_____
_____
_____
_____
_____
_____
_____
_____
_____

P – rayer: What do you need to say to God about the verse or passage?

_____
_____
_____
_____
_____
_____
_____
_____
_____

Space Pets

Interesting title? It is more than a title; it is the name of an acrostic developed by Pastor Rick Warren that can help you get more out of God's Word during your devotional time. Let's take a moment to look at it together.

Is there any...

S – Is there a sin to confess?

P – Is there a promise to claim?

A – Is there an attitude to change?

C – Is there a command to keep?

E – Is there an example to follow?

P – Is there a prayer to pray?

E – Is there an error to avoid?

T – Is there a truth to believe?

S – Is there something to thank God for?

Space Pets

S – Is there a sin to confess?

P – Is there a promise to claim?

A – Is there an attitude to change?

C – Is there a command to keep?

E – Is there an example to follow?

P – Is there a prayer to pray?

E – Is there an error to avoid?

T – Is there a truth to believe?

S – Is there something to thank God for?

CHAPTER 3

Biblical Study Methods

The Apostle Paul told Timothy something that is very applicable as we begin this study.

"Do your best to present yourself to God as one approved, a worker who does not need to be ashamed and who correctly handles the word of truth."
(2 Timothy 2:15)

He wanted his protégé to handle the Word of God correctly. This should be the desire of any man or woman who wants to preach. There is a way to do this and a way not to do this.

First, there should be a dependence on the Holy Spirit to prepare a message to preach.

"So he said to me, "This is the word of the Lord to Zerubbabel: 'Not by might nor by power, but by my Spirit,' says the Lord Almighty." (Zechariah 4:6)

1. Why is dependence on the Holy Spirit to prepare a message important?

_____

_____

_____

_____

_____

God can do in one second what a preacher could not achieve in a lifetime of trying. So, asking God to help you prepare the message is the best starting place. After all, it's His message, not ours. It's His Word, not ours. He is the author and knows how it is to be communicated with accuracy.

Second, the way in which the Word of God is approached to prepare a message is important. There are two ways to do this.

Exegesis – This is the practice of forming a belief from scripture alone.

Eisegesis – This is the practice of imposing one's own ideas, bias, or desires onto scripture.

2. Why is eisegesis dangerous when it comes to preaching?

_____
_____
_____
_____
_____

Our beliefs should come from Scripture alone.

"All Scripture is God-breathed and is useful for teaching, rebuking, correcting and training in righteousness, so that the servant of God may be thoroughly equipped for every good work." (2 Timothy 3:16-17)

Our preaching should come from scripture alone. Why? The Word of God will be handled correctly, and the truth will be delivered as God desires. Let's look at ways to prepare a sermon by exegesis.

On the following pages you will learn the Bible Study methods of:
- Verse by Verse: How to Study a Passage of the Bible Verse by Verse
- Thematic: How to Investigate the Themes of Scripture
- Character Quality: How to Determine Biblical Character Qualities
- Secondhand: Make a Christian Book Personal.

Verse by Verse Method: Example

How to Study a Passage of the Bible Verse by Verse

Verse	Different Translation
"It is actually reported that there is sexual immorality among you, and of a kind that even pagans do not tolerate: A man is sleeping with his father's wife." (1 Corinthians 5:1)	"I also received a report of scandalous sex within your church family, a kind that wouldn't be tolerated even outside the church: One of your men is sleeping with his stepmother." (1 Corinthians 5:1, MSG)

Questions	Cross-References
What is a pagan? In the Bible, the term "pagan" is generally used to describe individuals or groups who engage in practices that are outside the covenant relationship with God.	"You shall not uncover the nakedness of your father's wife; it is your father's nakedness." (Leviticus 18:8) "But sexual immorality and all impurity or covetousness must not even be named among you, as is proper among saints." (Ephesians 5:3)

Insights Learned	Personal Life Application
There was a man in the church of Corinth that was sleeping with his stepmom. This was even shocking to the unbelievers in the community.	We should remember that our sin can shock unbelievers and that is an undesirable result.

Verse	Different Translation
"And you are proud! Shouldn't you rather have gone into mourning and have put out of your fellowship the man who has been doing this?" (1 Corinthians 5:2)	"And you're so above it all that it doesn't even faze you! Shouldn't this break your hearts? Shouldn't it bring you to your knees in tears? Shouldn't this person and his conduct be confronted and dealt with?" (1 Corinthians 5:2, MSG)

Questions	Cross-References
What does it mean to put a man out of the fellowship? Paul commends them to remove the unrepentant sinner from their fellowship to preserve the church's holiness and lead to the person's spiritual change.	"God judges those outside. 'Purge the evil person from among you.'" (1 Corinthians 5:13) "My eyes shed streams of tears, because people do not keep your law." (Psalm 119:36)

Insights Learned	Personal Life Application
One of the goals of believers and churches should be to bring the saved and lost to repentance. It is not appropriate for a church or a believer to overlook sin and pretend it is okay.	As a pastor, I need to remember these things to help others deal with their sins and overcome them. I cannot ignore sin or it becomes an unacceptable norm never meant to be.

Verse by Verse Method:
How to Study a Passage of the Bible Verse by Verse

Verse	Different Translation

Questions	Cross-references

Insights Learned	Personal Life Application

Thematic Method: Example
How to Investigate the Themes of Scripture

1. Theme: **Jesus' Definition of a Disciple**

2. List of References:
   A. Matthew 10:24-25
   B. Luke 14:26-28
   C. Luke 14:33
   D. John 8:31-32
   E. John 13:34-35
   F. John 15:8
   G.

3. Questions to Be Asked:
   A. What are the characteristics of a disciple?
   B. What are the results of being a disciple?
   C.
   D.
   E.

4. Answers to Questions:
   A. Scripture Reference: Matthew 10:24-25

   1.) A disciple will be like Christ, his or her Master.

   2.) He or she should expect to be treated as Christ was by the world.

   3.)

   4.)

   5.)

B. Scripture Reference: Luke 14:26-28
   1.) A disciple's supreme love is Christ and bears his or her cross and follows Christ.

   2.)

   3.)

   4.)

   5.)

C. Scripture Reference: Luke 14:33
   1.) A disciple gives all to follow Christ.

   2.)

   3.)

   4.)

   5.)

D. Scripture Reference: John 8:31-32
   1.) A disciple continually abides in Christ's Word.

   2.) He knows the truth and is set free.

   3.)

   4.)

   5.)

E. Scripture Reference: John 13:34-35
   1.) A disciple has love for others.

   2.) Others will know that he or she belongs to Christ.

   3.)

   4.)

   5.)

F. Scripture Reference: John 15:8
   1.) A disciple bears fruit.

   2.) His or her bearing fruit brings glory to God.

   3.)

   4.)

   5.)

G. Scripture Reference:
   1.)

   2.)

   3.)

   4.)

   5.)

5. Conclusion

   A. Characteristics I discovered…

      1.) A disciple is like Christ.
      2.) A disciple gives supreme love to Christ.
      3.) A disciple bears his cross and follows Christ.
      4.) A disciple gives up all to follow Christ.
      5.) A disciple loves others.
      6.) A disciple bears fruit.

   B. Results I discovered…

      1.) He or she should expect persecution.
      2.) He or she knows the truth and is set free.
      3.) He or she brings glory to God.
      4.) Others notice he or she belongs to Christ.

6. Application

   A. Based on John 8:31-32, I will establish a regular, daily quiet time in the Word, starting tomorrow morning.

   B. Based on John 13:34-35, I will demonstrate love for the person in my neighborhood that I am impatient with and ask them and their family to dinner next week.

Thematic Method:
How to Investigate the Themes of Scripture

1. Theme:

2. List of References:

    A.

    B.

    C.

    D.

    E.

    F.

    G.

3. Questions to Be Asked:

    A.

    B.

    C.

    D.

    E.

4. Answers to Questions:
   A. Scripture Reference:
      1.)

      2.)

      3.)

      4.)

      5.)

   B. Scripture Reference:
      1.)

      2.)

      3.)

      4.)

      5.)

   C. Scripture Reference:
      1.)

      2.)

      3.)

      4.)

      5.)

D. Scripture Reference:
  1.)

  2.)

  3.)

  4.)

  5.)

E. Scripture Reference:

  1.)

  2.)

  3.)

  4.)

  5.)

F. Scripture Reference:
  1.)

  2.)

  3.)

  4.)

  5.)

G. Scripture Reference:

1.)

2.)

3.)

4.)

5.)

Character Quality Method: Example
How to Determine Biblical Character Qualities

1. Character Quality: Boldness

   A. Definition – An exhibition of courage and fearlessness; bravery; willingness to move ahead confidently in the face of danger.

2. Opposite Quality: Timidity; Fearfulness

   A. Definition – To shrink back from a difficult or dangerous circumstance; to be hesitant.

3. Simple Word Study:

   A. Old Testament word:

      1.) Batah means to be confident.
         a. Example – Proverbs 28:1 – "The righteous are as bold as a lion."

   B. New Testament words:

      1.) Tharreo means to be confident, bold, or daring.
         a. Example – Hebrews 13:6 – "So that we may boldly say, 'The Lord is my helper, and I will not fear what man shall do unto me.'"

      2.) Parrcsiazomai means to speak boldly or freely.
         a. Example – Acts 19:8 – "Paul entered the synagogue and spoke boldly there for three months, arguing persuasively about the kingdom of God."

C. Reference Tools Used:

    1.) Young's Analytical Concordance to the Bible

    2.) Vine's Expository Dictionary of New Testament Words

4. Cross-Reference Insights:

A. Christ spoke boldly in the face of opposition (John 7:26).
B. Our confidence and boldness come from knowing that the Lord will help us in difficult situations (Hebrews 13:6).
C. Peter and John were bold because they had been with Jesus (Acts 4:13).
D. When the Holy Spirit fills our life, we will be able to speak the Word of God boldly. The first Christians prayed for boldness in witnessing and God answered their prayer by filling them with the Holy Spirit (Acts 4:29-31).
E. When Christ's love is in us, we will be bold because there is no fear in love. Perfect love casts out all fear (1 John 4:17-18).

5. Simple Biographical Study:

A. The Apostle Paul is a major example of boldness. His entire life seemed to be characterized by this quality.

    1.) As a young Christian in Damascus, he witnessed boldly for Christ (Acts 9:27).
    2.) Everywhere he went, he shared his faith boldly in spite of opposition and persecution.
        A.)   In Jerusalem (Acts 9:28-29)
        B.)   In Pisidian Antioch (Acts 13:45)
        C.)   In Iconium (Acts 14:3)
        D.)   In Ephesus (Acts 19:8)
        E.)   In Thessalonica (1 Thessalonians 2:2)

3.) He wrote bold letters to the churches (Romans 15:15).

4.) He asked people to pray that he would continually preach and teach with boldness (Ephesians 6:19-20).

5.) His Christian testimony while in prison caused others to speak boldly for Christ (Philippians 1:14).

6.) He even faced death boldly (Philippians 1:20).

6. Memory Verses:

A. "So we say with confidence. 'The Lord is my helper; I will not be afraid. What can man do to me?" (Hebrews 13:6)

7. Situation or Relationship (where God wants to work on this quality in my life):

A. I have been afraid to witness to my friend Ted, who works with me at the office.

8. My Project:

A. I will ask Robert to pray with me about overcoming my timidity in witnessing to Ted. Then each day this week I will praise before going into the office and ask to be filled with the Holy Spirit to give me boldness to witness (Acts 4:31).

9. Personal Illustration:

   I asked Robert to start interceding for me to have an opportunity to share my faith with Ted and have boldness. I also began to pray every day to be filled with the Holy Spirit when I went into work. Ted came to me one day during lunch and asked to talk to me. He told me that he had noticed my Bible and wanted to talk about it. I knew that the prayers of Robert had worked and that God would give me boldness to talk to Ted. That day started many days of Ted wanting to talk about God and my opportunity to share with him. I look forward to those days and plan to share the Gospel as we are studying the salvation chapter of Romans 10 tomorrow!

Character Quality Method:
How to Determine Biblical Character Qualities

1. Character Quality:

   A. Definition –

2. Opposite Quality:

   A. Definition –

3. Simple Word Study:

4. Cross-Reference Insights:

5. Simple Biographical Study:

6. Memory Verses:

7. Situation or Relationship (where God wants to work on this quality in my life):

8. My Project:

9. Personal Illustration:

Secondhand Method:
Make a Christian Book Personal

The Bible says, *"Then Jesus came to them and said, 'All authority in heaven and on earth has been given to me. Therefore go and make disciples of all nations, baptizing them in the name of the Father and of the Son and of the Holy Spirit, and teaching them to obey everything I have commanded you. And surely I am with you always, to the very end of the age.'" (Matthew 28:18-20)*

1. What are we supposed to make?

_____

_____

_____

_____

_____

Making disciples is easier than it has ever been due to the availability of Christian books and Bible studies. You may never meet Rick Warren, David Jeremiah, John Maxwell, or Billy Graham, but you can read what they have authored! In essence, they are discipling you.

One of my Bible College professors, Dr. Gene Brown, taught us that the pastor who reads will always have something to preach! We need to let other men and women of God, past and present, disciple us. They are fulfilling what the Apostle Paul told Timothy by their writings.

"You then, my son, be strong in the grace that is in Christ Jesus. And the things you have heard me say in the presence of many witnesses entrust to reliable people who will also be qualified to teach others." (2 Timothy 2:1-2)

There will be times that you are reading, and you might think, "That will preach!" God may just tell you that you are the one to pass it on to others.

2. Is there anything that you ever read in a Christian book and wanted to tell someone about it? What was it?

_____

_____

_____

_____

_____

The following is an excerpt from one of my favorite authors who writes commentaries. Warren Weirsbe is one who is easy to create a sermon outline from and make it personal. Look it over and see if you could find an outline.

CHAPTER TWO
Jude 8–16
MEET THE APOSTATES!

Jude was not content simply to remind his readers to pay attention to what Peter had written. He wanted to add his own words of warning by describing what the false teachers were like and what they would do to the church. The Spirit of God led Jude to describe the characteristics of the apostates, reinforcing Peter's words and, at the same time, adding information. Jude 8–16 and 2 Peter 2 parallel and supplement each other.

But why this seemingly needless repetition? The apostle Paul gave the answer: "To write the same things to you, to me indeed is not grievous, but for you it is safe" (Phil. 3:1). Parents repeat warnings and instructions to their children, and sometimes the children reply, "I know that! You've already told me a million times!" But wise parents know that some things must be said again and again for the safety and welfare of their children—whether the children want to hear them or not! All that Jude wrote about the apostates in these verses may be summarized in three statements.

They Reject Divine Authority (8–11) - All authority comes from the throne of God, whether it is authority in the home, the church, or the state. Those who exercise authority must first be under authority, accountable to God. But the false teachers reject divine authority and set themselves up as their own authority.

The cause of their rebellion is found in the word dreamers (Jude 8). These people live in a dream world of unreality and delusion. They believe Satan's lie, "Ye shall be as gods" (Gen. 3:5). Having turned away from God's truth, they feed their minds on false doctrine that inflates their egos and encourages their rebellion. Jude 10 informs us that the apostates are ignorant people who do not know what they are talking about! Jude echoed Peter's description of these men as "brute beasts" (2 Peter 2:12, 22). Animals live by natural instinct, and so do the apostates. When men rebel against God, they sink to the level of beasts.

The course of their rebellion was clearly described by Jude. As a result of their rebellion and pride, they "defile the flesh," living to satisfy their animal lusts. When a person despises God's authority, he feels free to disobey God's laws and live as he pleases. What he for gets is that those laws have penalties attached to them so that he cannot disobey and escape the consequences.

They also use their tongues to express their rebel lion against God. "With our tongue will we prevail; our lips are our own: who is lord over us?" (Ps. 12:4). The phrase, speak evil, in Jude 8 and 10 simply means "to blaspheme." Blasphemy involves much more than taking God's name in vain, though that is at the heart of it. A person blasphemes God when he takes His Word lightly and even jests about it, or when he deliberately defies God to judge him. "They set their mouth against the heavens, and their tongue walketh through the earth. And they say, 'How doth God know? and is there knowledge in the Most High?'" (Ps. 73:9, 11).

The consequence of their rebellion is seen in their own ruin: "they corrupt [destroy] themselves" (Jude 10). They defile themselves (Jude 8) and they destroy themselves, yet they have the idea they are promoting themselves! "Because sentence against an evil work is not executed speedily, therefore the heart of the sons of men is fully set in them to do evil" (Eccl. 8:11). The way of rebellion is but the way to ruin.

Arrogant speech is a dangerous thing, and so is despising the authority that God has established. Even the archangel Michael (Dan. 10:13) did not dare to rebuke Satan, but respected the authority given to him by God. The name Michael means "Who is like God?" Ironically, Satan had said in his rebellion, "I will be like the Most High!" (Isa. 14:14), and his offer to men is, "Ye shall be as gods" (Gen. 3:5).

We have no information about the conflict between Satan and Michael over the body of Moses. When Moses died, the Lord buried him and no one knew where the sepulcher was located (Deut. 34:5–6). No doubt the Jewish people would have made a shrine out 1026 Jude of the sepulcher and fallen into idolatry, so God kept the information to Himself. The text tells us that "not any man" knew the place, so perhaps Satan did know the place and tried to claim Moses' body for himself. Inasmuch as Satan does have a certain amount of authority in the realm of death he may have felt he had a right to interfere (Heb. 2:14–15).

The point is that Michael did not rebuke Satan, but left that to the Lord. It is a dangerous thing for God's people to confront Satan directly and to argue with him, because he is much stronger than we are. If an archangel is careful about the way he deals with the devil, how much more cautious ought we to be! While it is true that we share in the victory of Christ, it is also true that we must not be presumptuous. Satan is a dangerous enemy, and when we resist him, we must be sober and vigilant (1 Peter 5:8–9).

"The Lord rebuke thee!" has a parallel in Zechariah 3:1–5. The prophet had a vision of the high priest standing before God's throne in defiled garments, symbolizing the sinful condition of the nation Israel after the Babylonian captivity. Satan had every right to accuse the people (see Rev. 12:9–11), except for one thing: they were the chosen ones of God, His covenant people, and He would not go back on His Word. God forgave His people, gave them clean garments, and warned them to walk in His ways. This is an Old Testament illustration of 1 John 1:5–2:2.

The condemnation of the false teachers is given in Jude 11: "Woe unto them!" Jude cited three examples from the Old Testament to illustrate the enormity of their sins, three men who rebelled against God's authority and who suffered for it.

Cain rebelled against God's way of salvation (Gen. 4; 1 John 3:11–12). By clothing Adam and Eve with the skins of slain animals (Gen. 3:21), God made it clear that the only way of forgiveness is through the shedding of blood. This is the way of faith, not the way of good works (Eph. 2:8–10). But Cain rejected this divinely authorized way and came to the altar with the fruits of his own labor. God rejected Cain's offering because God rejected Cain: his heart was not right before God. It was by faith that Abel's sacrifice was offered, and that was why God accepted it (Heb. 11:4).

The "way of Cain" is the way of religion without faith, righteousness based on character and good works. The "way of Cain" is the way of pride, a man establishing his own righteousness and rejecting the righteousness of God that comes through faith in Christ (Rom. 10:1–4; Phil. 3:3–12). Cain became a fugitive and tried to overcome his wretchedness by building a city and developing a civilization (Gen. 4:9ff.). He ended up with everything a man could desire, everything, that is, except God.

We have already studied "the way of Balaam" (see 2 Peter 2:15–16). The "way of Balaam" is merchandising one's gifts and ministry just for the purpose of making money. It is using the spiritual to gain the material (see 1 Thess. 2:5–6; 1 Tim. 6:3–21). The false teachers were greedy for material gain and, like Balaam, would do anything for money. The "error of Balaam" is thinking that they can get away with this kind of rebellion. Balaam was a true prophet of God, but he prostituted his gifts and sought to destroy God's people. God turned Balaam's curses into blessings (Deut. 23:4–5).

While we are on the subject of Balaam, we might note the "doctrine of Balaam" (Rev. 2:14), which is, "You can violate your separated position and get away with it!" He told King Balak that the fastest way to destroy Israel would be to corrupt the nation by having the people defile themselves with the heathen nations around them. "You are God's chosen people," was the argument. "Certainly, a little friendship with your neighbors will not hurt you!" It was "turning the grace of… God into lasciviousness" (Jude 4), and God judged both Israel and Balaam.

The story of Core (Korah) is found in Numbers 16, and it too centers on rebellion against authority. Korah and his followers resented the leadership of Moses and dared God to do anything about their rebellion. In speaking against ("gainsaying") Moses, they were speaking against the Lord who had given Moses his authority. This is a warning to us today, for it is so easy to speak against spiritual or governmental leaders in a careless way (see Titus 3:1–2). God judged Korah and his followers and established clearly the authority of His servant, Moses.

Cain rebelled against God's authority in salvation, for he refused to bring a blood sacrifice as God had commanded. Balaam rebelled against God's authority in separation, for he prostituted his gifts for money and led Israel to mix with the other nations. Korah rebelled against God's authority in service, denying that Moses was God's appointed servant and attempting to usurp his authority. It is interesting to note the verbs that Jude used in this verse. The apostates "traveled on the road" of Cain, "gave themselves over to" the error of Balaam, and "perished" in the rebellion of Korah. The tragedy of rejecting authority!

They Resort to Deliberate Hypocrisy (12–13, 16) - Jude 12 and 13 present six vivid pictures of the false teachers and help to explain why they are dangerous to the church.

Filthy spots (v. 12a). Peter called them spots and blemishes (2 Peter 2:13). These men had invaded the "love feasts" in the local assemblies, but all they did was defile them. Instead of adding to the sanctity of the occasion, they detracted from it, like Judas at the last Passover that Jesus celebrated with His disciples. The tragedy is that the members of the assembly did not realize the true character of these men! They thought the men were spiritual!

The Greek word translated "spots" can also mean "hidden rocks." The mariner who is unaware of the hidden rocks can quickly wreck his ship. The pilot must always be alert, for waters that look calm and safe can contain treacherous reefs. Spiritual leaders must constantly be on guard.

Selfish shepherds (v. 12b). The word translated "feeding" means "shepherding." Instead of shepherding the flock and caring for the needs of the people, these apostates only take care of themselves. Jude may have had in mind Isaiah 56:10–12 and Ezekiel 34, where the prophets condemned the political and spiritual leaders of the nation ("shepherds") for exploiting the people and caring only for themselves.

It is a serious thing to be a shepherd over God's flock. Our example must be Jesus Christ, the Good Shepherd who gave His life for the sheep. False shepherds use and abuse people in order to get what they want, and yet all the while, the people love it! Paul marveled at this when he wrote 2 Corinthians 11:20— "You don't mind, do you, if a man takes away your liberty, spends your money, takes advantage of you, puts on airs, or even smacks your face?" (ph).

These selfish shepherds do all of this "without fear." They are an arrogant lot! This is the difference between a true shepherd and a hireling: the true shepherd cares for the sheep, while the hireling cares only for himself. "Woe be to the shepherds of Israel that do feed themselves! Should not the shepherds feed the flocks?" (Ezek. 34:2). But these apostates ought to be afraid, for their judgment is coming.

Empty clouds (v. 12c). Clouds that promise rain, but fail to produce, are a disappointment to the farmer whose crops desperately need water. The apostates look like men who can give spiritual help, and they boast of their abilities, but they are unable to produce. "Whoso boasteth himself of a false gift [a gift he does not give] is like clouds and wind without rain" (Prov. 25:14). They promise liberty, but they can only give bondage (2 Peter 2:19).

The Word of God is sometimes compared to the rain and the dew. "My doctrine shall drop as the rain, my speech shall distill as the dew" (Deut. 32:2). Isaiah 55:10 compares God's Word to the rain and snow from heaven that bring fruit on the earth. Like the clouds in the sky, the false teachers may be prominent and even attractive, but if they cannot bring rain, they are useless.

Dead trees (v. 12d). The picture is that of an orchard in autumn, the time when the farmer expects fruit. But these trees are fruitless! "Ye shall know them by their fruits" (Matt. 7:16). Those who teach and preach the Word have the responsibility of feeding oth ers, but the false teachers have nothing to give. Not only are they fruitless, but they are also rootless ("plucked up by the root"); this is why they are "twice dead." What a contrast to the godly man in Psalm 1:3!

One of the evidences of true salvation is producing spiritual fruit. The seed that fell on the hard soil, the shallow soil, and the crowded soil did not produce fruit, but the seed that fell on the "good ground" did produce fruit (Matt. 13:1–9, 18–23). No matter how much of the Bible the false teachers may quote, the seed is not producing fruit in their own lives or through their ministries. Why? Because they have no spiritual roots. They lack spiritual life.

Fruit has in it the seed for more fruit (Gen. 1:11–12). One of the evidences that a ministry is truly of God is that the fruit multiplies. Manufactured "results" are sterile and dead, but true fruit continues to grow and reproduce itself in the lives of others.

Raging waves (v, 13a). I personally do not enjoy being in or on the ocean (I am not a good swimmer). However, I do enjoy sitting by the ocean and contemplating its grandeur and power. But I certainly would not want to be either in or on the ocean in a storm! There is great power in those waves, as many a mariner has discovered. But Jude compared the apostates to "raging waves of the sea" not because of their power, but because of their pride and arrogant speech. "Their mouth speaketh great swelling words" (Jude 16). Like the swelling of the sea, they make a lot of noise, but what do they produce? Have you ever walked along the beach the morning after a storm and seen the ugly refuse that has been deposited on the shore?

Jude may have had Isaiah 57:20 in mind: "But the wicked are like the troubled sea, when it cannot rest, whose waters cast up mire and dirt." All that the "great swelling words" of the apostates can produce is foam and flotsam! The true teachers of the Word bring up the treasures of the deep, but the false teachers produce only refuse. And what they boast about, they really ought to be ashamed of (see Phil. 3:19)!

Wandering stars (v. 13b). Jude was not referring to fixed stars, planets, or comets, because they have definite positions and orbits. He was referring to meteors, falling stars that suddenly appear and then vanish into the darkness, never to be seen again. Our Lord is compared to a star (Rev. 2:28; 22:16), and Christians are to shine as stars in this dark world (Phil. 2:15). Fixed stars can be depended on to guide the traveler through the darkness, but wandering stars can only lead him astray.

One of my hobbies is collecting books of sermons, not only by famous preachers, but also by obscure and forgotten men whose names once were famous. I have noticed that many a "pulpit beacon" has turned out to be a fallen star! It is disturbing to read histories and biographies and see how "the mighty have fallen." For the most part, those who have been true to the Word are ministering yet today as lights shining in the dark ness, while the preachers of false doctrine have fallen into oblivion.

God has reserved chains of darkness for the rebellious angels (Jude 6), and He has reserved "the blackness of darkness forever" for apostate teachers. Beware of following a falling star! It will lead you into eternal blackness!

As you review these six pictures of the false teachers, you can easily see how dangerous they are and how important it is for the church to keep them out.

Murmurers and complainers (v. 16). Jude 16 completes the description and emphasizes even more why they are so dangerous: they are out to please themselves by taking advantage of others. This reminds us of Peter's statement (2 Peter 2:14), "A heart they have exercised with covetous practices" or, as Phillips trans lates it, "Their technique of getting what they want is, through long practice, highly developed." They give the impression that they are out to help you, but they are interested only in gratifying their own lusts.

What is their approach? For one thing, they murmur and complain and cause people to become dissatisfied with life. While each of us should do all we can, as God enables us, to improve our lot in life, at the same time we must be careful not to criticize God's providences or hinder His plans. The nation of Israel was judged because of her complaining (1 Cor. 10:1–10), and Christians are commanded not to complain (Phil. 2:14–16). If a false teacher can make a person critical of his pastor or church, or dissatisfied with his situation, he then can lead him astray into false doctrine.

The false teachers also use "great swelling words" to impress ignorant people. Peter called their speeches "great swelling words of vanity" (2 Peter

2:18). They impress people with their vocabularies and oratory, but what they say is just so much "hot air." They also use flattery to manipulate their listeners. They "bow and scrape" and pay compliments to others, if it is to their advantage.

Knowing these things, we are amazed that anybody would listen to these apostates and follow them, but many people are doing it today! There is something in fallen human nature that loves a lie and is willing to follow it, no matter where it may lead. But the success of the apostates is only temporary, for their judgment is coming.

They Receive Their Due Penalty (14–15) – All that we know about Enoch from Scripture is found in Genesis 5:18–24; Hebrews 11:5; and these two verses in Jude. He is called "the seventh from Adam" to identify him as the godly Enoch, since Cain had a son of the same name (Gen. 4:17). In a society that was rapidly being polluted and destroyed by sin, Enoch walked with God and kept his life clean. He also ministered as a prophet and announced the coming judgment.

Bible scholars tell us that this quotation is from an apocryphal book called The Book of Enoch. The fact that Jude quoted from this nonbiblical book does not mean the book is inspired and trustworthy, any more than Paul's quotations from the Greek poets put God's "seal of approval" on everything they wrote. The Spirit of God led Jude to use this quotation and make it a part of the inspired Scriptures. When Enoch originally gave this message, it is possible that he was also referring to the coming judgment of the flood. He certainly lived in an ungodly age, and it seemed that sinners were getting away with their evil deeds. But Enoch made it clear that judgment was coming and that the ungodly would get what was coming to them!

However, the final application of this prophecy is to the world in the end times, the very judgment that Peter wrote about in 2 Peter 3. The false teachers mocked this prophecy and argued that Jesus Christ would never come and God would never send judgment. But their very attitude was proof that the Word is true, for both our Lord and His apostles, as well as the prophets, said that scoffers and mockers would appear in the last days (2 Peter 3:1–4). Enoch gave his prophecy thousands of years ago! See how patient God has been with those who have rebelled against Him!

What does Enoch's prophecy say about the coming judgment? It will be a personal judgment: God Himself will come to judge the world. He will not send a famine or a flood, nor will He assign the task to an angel. He Himself will come. This shows the serious ness of the event, and also its finality. "Behold, the Judge standeth before the door" (James 5:9).

Though it is a personal judgment, our Lord will not judge alone; the saints of God will be with Him. The word saints in Jude 14 means "holy ones" and can also refer to the angels (Deut. 33:2; Matt. 25:31). However, we know from Revelation 19:14; Colossians 3:4; and 1 Thessalonians 3:13 that the people of God will accompany the Lord when He returns to earth to defeat His enemies and establish His righteous kingdom (cf. 1 Cor. 6:2–3). Over the centuries, the people of God have suffered at the hands of the ungodly, but one day the tables will be turned.

It will be a universal judgment. He will execute judgment "upon all"— none will escape. Just as the flood destroyed all who were outside the ark, and the fire and brimstone destroyed all in Sodom and Gomorrah except Lot and his wife and two daughters, so the last judgment will encompass all the ungodly. The word ungodly is used four times in this one verse! It will be "the day of judgment and perdition [ruin, destruction] of ungodly men" (2 Peter 3:7).

It will be a just judgment. God will convict ("convince") them of their sins, declare them guilty, pass sentence on them, and then execute the punishment. There will be a Judge, Jesus Christ (John 5:22), but no jury. There will be prosecution, but no defense, for every mouth will be stopped (Rom. 3:19). There will be a sentence, but no appeal, for there can be no higher court than God's final judgment. The entire procedure will be just, for the righteous Son of God will be in charge.

The Lord will have the record of their "ungodly deeds." He will also have a record of their motives and hidden desires as they committed these deeds and even these will be ungodly! He will recall the "hard speeches" (Jude 15) that they uttered against the Lord. The word hard carries the idea of "rough, harsh, stem, uncivil." After all, these people were "murmurers" and "complainers" (Jude 16) and spoke harsh things against God. They were not "afraid to speak evil of dignities" 1029 Jude (2 Peter 2:10), but at the judgment their words will testify against them. They spoke "great swelling words" (2 Peter 2:18; Jude 16), but at the judgment their great words will bring great wrath.

There are times when God's children ask, "Lord, how long shall the wicked, how long shall the wicked triumph? How long shall they utter and speak hard things? and all the workers of iniquity boast them selves?" (Ps. 94:3–4). The answer is given in Psalm 50:3—"Our God shall come, and shall not keep silence: a fire shall devour before him, and it shall be very tempestuous round about him."

The words are familiar, but what James Russell Lowell wrote in "The Present Crisis" certainly applies today.

Careless seems the great Avenger; history's pages but record One death-grapple in the darkness 'twix old systems and the Word; Truth forever on the scaffold, Wrong forever on the throne— Yet that scaffold sways the future, and, behind the dim unknown, Standeth God within the shadow, keeping watch above His own…. "Nevertheless we, according to His promise, look for new heavens and a new earth, wherein dwelleth righteousness" (2 Peter 3:13). "Even so, come, Lord Jesus!"[2]

---

[2] https://bethelchurchmuncie.wordpress.com/wp-content/uploads/2020/07/wiersbe-commentary-new-testament.pdf

From this inspirational commentary, there is rich Biblical study and an outline. The below outline and some of the commentary could be used along with adding your own personal touches to preach an expository message on Jude 8-16.

Meet the Apostates

1. They reject divine authority (Jude 8-11).

2. They resort to deliberate hypocrisy (Jude 12-13, 16).

    A. Filthy spots (Jude 12a).
    B. Selfish shepherds (Jude 12b).
    C. Empty clouds (Jude 12c).
    D. Dead trees (Jude 12d).
    E. Raging waves (Jude 13a).
    F. Wandering stars (Jude 13b).
    G. Murmuring and complainers (Jude 16).

3. They receive their due penalty (Jude 14-15).

CHAPTER 4

Sermon Styles

Have you ever taken a personality test? There are many exciting ones to take and one which stands out to me is the DiSC Profile. The following are the different personality types according to this test.

D = Dominance

People with the DiSC D style personality are usually direct, driven, and results oriented. You'll notice the D style acting assertively, making quick decisions, and speaking candidly.[3]

I = Influence

A person in this DiSC quadrant places emphasis on influencing or persuading others. They tend to be enthusiastic, optimistic, open, trusting, and energetic.

S = Steadiness

A person in this DiSC quadrant places emphasis on cooperation, sincerity, loyalty, and dependability. They tend to have calm, deliberate dispositions, and don't like to be rushed.

---

[3] https://www.discprofile.com/disc-styles

C = Conscientiousness

A person in this DiSC quadrant places emphasis on quality and accuracy, expertise and competency. They enjoy their independence, demand the details, and often fear being wrong.

Which one do you most identify with? What about the second? Most people are a combination of two traits.

Just as there are different personalities, there are different ways to outline a sermon. You can use one or all! I have utilized multiple sermon outlining techniques over the years. This chapter will introduce four different ways for you to consider.

SERMON OUTLINING - FOUR DIFFERENT WAYS

1. The Rhetorical Sermon: All Available Ways of Persuasion
2. The Relational Sermon: Having a Conversation
3. The Declarative Sermon: Make an Argument
4. The Pragmatic Sermon: Solve a Mystery

The Rhetorical Sermon:
All Available Ways of Persuasion

Rhetoric is designed to influence or persuade others. It is building an argument to prove a point. To accomplish this, four questions need to be answered.

1. Explanation: What is the meaning of this verse?
2. Argumentation: How do you know that is the meaning?
3. Illustration: What does it look like? Can you give me a concrete example?
4. Application: What does this have to do with my life?

These four questions need to be asked of every sermon point.

Here is an example…

Let's use the following passage to develop an outline.

"1 You then, my son, be strong in the grace that is in Christ Jesus. 2 And the things you have heard me say in the presence of many witnesses entrust to reliable people who will also be qualified to teach others. 3 Join with me in suffering, like a good soldier of Christ Jesus. 4 No one serving as a soldier gets entangled in civilian affairs, but rather tries to please his commanding officer. 5 Similarly, anyone who competes as an athlete does not receive the victor's crown except by competing according to the rules. 6 The hardworking farmer should be the first to receive a share of the crops. 7 Reflect on what I am saying, for the Lord will give you insight into all this." (2 Timothy 2:1-7)

NOTE: Please keep the following in mind as you develop sermon outlines. A 7-page outline with single spacing (except between points) will give you at least 30 minutes of speaking material. A 10-page outline will give you at least 45 minutes of speaking material.

Be Strong in God's Grace

I. Introduction

1. Do you know who the strongest man in the world was?

   A. The strongest man in the world according to historical records is Paul Anderson, who set several world records in weightlifting during the 1950s. He achieved remarkable feats, including lifting a total of 762.25 lb (345.8 kg) in 1953, which is often cited as one of the greatest feats of strength in history.

   B. It is one thing to be physically strong, but the strength that really matters to God is spiritual strength.

2. The Apostle Paul said, *"You then, my son, be strong in the grace that is in Christ Jesus."* (2 Timothy 2:1)

   A. Strongness comes from God's grace!

   B. What can we do by God's grace?

II. Body

1. First, be strong in God's grace and entrust to others what God taught you (2 Timothy 2:2).

   A. *"2 And the things you have heard me say in the presence of many witnesses entrust to reliable people who will also be qualified to teach others."* (2 Timothy 2:2)

1.) What is the meaning of this verse? (Give the answer)

2.) How do you know that is the meaning (Give the answer)

3.) What does it look like? Can you give me a concrete example? (Give the answer)

4.) What does this have to do with my life? (Give the answer)

2. Next, be strong in God's grace by being a good soldier (2 Timothy 2:3-4).

A. *"Join with me in suffering, like a good soldier of Christ Jesus. No one serving as a soldier gets entangled in civilian affairs, but rather tries to please his commanding officer."* (2 Timothy 2:3-4)

1.) What is the meaning of this verse? (Give the answer)

2.) How do you know that is the meaning? (Give the answer)

3.) What does it look like? Can you give me a concrete example? (Give the answer)

4.) What does this have to do with my life? (Give the answer)

3. Third, be strong in God's grace by competing according to the rules (2 Timothy 2:5).

A. *"Similarly, anyone who competes as an athlete does not receive the victor's crown except by competing according to the rules."* (2 Timothy 2:5)

1.) What is the meaning of this verse? (Give the answer)

2.) How do you know that is the meaning? (Give the answer)

3.) What does it look like? Can you give me a concrete example? (Give the answer)

4.) What does this have to do with my life? (Give the answer)

4. Last, be strong in God's grace by being a hard worker (2 Timothy 2:6).

A. *"The hardworking farmer should be the first to receive a share of the crops."* (2 Timothy 2:6)

   1.) What is the meaning of this verse? (Give the answer)

   2.) How do you know that is the meaning? (Give the answer)

   3.) What does it look like? Can you give me a concrete example? (Give the answer)

   4.) What does this have to do with my life? (Give the answer)

III. Conclusion

1. As we conclude this message, here are some quotes on spiritual strength.

   A. "Do not strive in your own strength; cast yourself at the feet of the Lord Jesus, and wait upon Him in the sure confidence that He is with you, and works in you. Strive in prayer; let faith fill your heart - so will you be strong in the Lord, and in the power of His might." (Andrew Murray)

   B. "When a man has no strength, if he leans on God, he becomes powerful." (D.L. Moody)

   C. "Once more, never think that you can live to God by your own power or strength; but always look to and rely on him for assistance, yea, for all strength and grace." (David Brainard)

2. The Apostle Paul lastly said, "7 Reflect on what I am saying, for the Lord will give you insight into all this." (2 Timothy 2:7).

3. Today we learned that God's grace gives us strength! It enables us to pass on what God taught us to others, be a good soldier for Christ, follow the rules, and work hard!

4. As this song plays, I want to invite you to come to the altar and ask God to give you strength by His grace!

The Relational Sermon:
Having a Conversation

I became aware of this style of sermon delivery after reading the book Communicating for a Change by Andy Stanley in 2006. It is one that focuses on helping people remember what you spoke about by concise point.

The traditional sermon consists of introduction, body, and conclusion. The relational sermon consists of me, we, God, you, and we.

What are the five parts?

1. **ME** (Orientation) – Introduce yourself and your topic – find common ground with your audience.

2. **WE** (Identification) – Build an emotional common ground with your audience – build as many bridges emotionally as possible.

3. **GOD** (Illumination) – God has a solution for us today – engage your audience with the text – don't just read it. Don't explain it to death. Make it fascinating!

4. **YOU** (Application) – Find one point of application everyone can embrace. Don't ask them to make a life-altering decision. Give them a measurable or reachable goal. Encourage them to try something for a week, a day, or even a month.

5. **WE** (Inspiration) – cast a vision – prompt a decision by briefly describing what would happen if this group of people would follow what has been taught. Tell them to imagine what WE could do together.[4]

The following would be a short example of this type of sermon outlining, but to speak for 30 to 45 minutes, it would need to be longer.

When God Whispers Your Name

I. Me

1. Many years ago, I was youth pastoring at Springs of Life Evangel Assembly, and it was youth service night! I made all my rounds of picking up kids and we arrived at the church.

   A. The students who did worship took their place and suddenly, the power went out at the church. Oops! How do you do worship in the dark? We got into a circle on the floor and sat down. I got a candle and put it in the middle of us all.

   B. One by one students began to sing worship songs without instruments, and it was amazing to see everyone participate. The worship was so powerful that God's presence could be felt in the room.

2. God ministered to the students in personal ways, and it was a service I will never forget. I want to experience more worship times like that! The power does not have to be out for it to happen.

---

[4] https://joshweidmann.com/me-we-god-you-we/

II. We

1. What about you? Do you want to experience the presence of God in that way?

2. Do you want to create an environment that is rich with the possibility of the Holy Spirit moving?

3. A place where God can whisper your name?

4. It has to do with all of us when we assemble together for a church service. Many years ago, there was a movie called, "Field of Dreams." A voice tells Kevin Costner to plow down his crops and build a baseball field. If he does that, Shoeless Joe Jackson will come from the grace. He builds it and Shoeless Joe and other baseball players from beyond come as the voice said.

5. If you build it (worship in unity), He (the Holy Spirit) will come.

    A. *"Now in the church at Antioch there were prophets and teachers: Barnabas, Simeon called Niger, Lucius of Cyrene, Manaen (who had been brought up with Herod the tetrarch) and Saul. While they were worshiping the Lord and fasting, the Holy Spirit said, 'Set apart for me Barnabas and Saul for the work to which I have called them.' So after they had fasted and prayed, they placed their hands on them and sent them off."* (Acts 13:1-3)

III. God

1. First, if you build it, the Holy Spirit will come: Unity (Acts 13:1-2a).

   A. *"Now in the church at Antioch there were prophets and teachers: Barnabas, Simeon called Niger, Lucius of Cyrene, Manaen (who had been brought up with Herod the tetrarch) and Saul. While they were worshiping the Lord and fasting..."* (Acts 13:1-2a)

   B. This echoes the unity found on the day of Pentecost when the 120 were in the upper room in one accord. No! We are not talking about a Honda.

   C. Everyone there was in unity! They united to worship and fast to seek the Lord.

   D. The prophets weren't talking among themselves while the teachers and the Apostle Paul worshipped. They all worshipped!

   E. Whenever a church assembles to worship, you need to join in and not be a spectator. It is an opportunity love on Jesus! He loved us first and enabled us to love Him back. He wants our love.

   F. Worshipping with others is a way to love the Lord God with all your heart, mind, soul, and body. It fulfills the greatest commandment.

2. Next, if you build it, the Holy Spirit will come: Power (Acts 13:2b-3).

   A. *"...the Holy Spirit said, 'Set apart for me Barnabas and Saul for the work to which I have called them.' So after they had fasted and prayed, they placed their hands on them and sent them off."* (Acts 13:2a-3)

B. Remember the phrase, "First comes love, then comes marriage?" The saying is about order.

C. A congregation worshipping together in unity has laid the groundwork for the Holy Spirit to show up in power.

D. This happened with the prophets, teachers, Paul, and Barnabus in Antioch. They worshipped and then the Holy Spirit spoke a prophetic word. What?

E. Paul and Barnabus were to be set apart to be a team to go on their first missionary journey together! Ready! Set! Go! Can you imagine knowing what God wanted you to do and the strength it would give.

F. *"But thou art holy, O thou that inhabitest the praises of Israel."* (Psalm 22:3, KJV)

G. God inhabits praise!

H. The Holy Spirit has the environment to show up in unified praise to give words of wisdom, words of knowledge, prophecy, discernment, healing, miracles, tongues, and interpretation!

I. I want that! Don't you? A church that does not go through the motions and be predictable, but one where God can show up and move spontaneously.

IV. You

1. The Bible is meant to be applied to life, so we need to apply "if you build it, the Holy Spirit will come" personally.

   A. Decide ahead of time before you ever get to church, you are going to participate in worship instead of being a spectator.

2. Watch and see what God does!

V. We

1. Imagine with me what took place recently in Sunday church services. We worshipped in unity and…

   A. Someone decided to get saved and water baptized.

   B. Then someone else decided to get saved and water baptized.

   C. Then someone came forward and got saved and God healed them of their blindness!

2. Let's keep worshipping in unity and come expectant to see what God will do.

In preaching this message, the speaker made the message personal to their own experience, not putting themselves above the congregation, and had a main point to remember. What was it? **If you build it, the Holy Spirit will come.** That is the point. Make it so your point will be remembered!

The Declarative Sermon:
Making an Argument

This is the style of sermon that I was taught at Southwestern Assemblies of God University in my preaching class and the type of sermons I delivered in my preaching lab to be evaluated. It is also the most common form of preaching among ministers.

Like a lawyer, the preacher arranges facts and puts the case before the people in the most convincing manner possible. It is presenting an argument and proving it. Here are some steps to use to develop a declarative sermon.[5]

1. Pray

You are wanting to hear what God has to say to you, and through you, to share with others. The message is God's message, so you need to hear from God. He knows totally about the people you will speak to and their lives. He can do in one second what you could not achieve in a lifetime. Therefore, developing a sermon starts with God. Ask Him to guide you! Ask for it to be His Word through you!

2. Choose Your Text

The Holy Spirit will point out to you what He wants you to preach on. It will be highlighted to you and you cannot seem to get away from it. I have found for myself that the things I preach on are the things I get excited about and think, "That will preach!" I can't wait to share it with others. It can be something God brings you back to over and over until you share it. The text

---

[5] Anderson, Kenton C, Choosing to Preach: A Comprehensive Introduction to Sermon Options and Structures: Grand Rapids. Michigan 49530 USA, Zondervan, 2006, page 133.

could be a passage of Scripture, a chapter of the Bible, a verse, a single verse that can be broken down into several points, a topic with the supporting scriptures, or you may even do a sermon series through a book of the Bible or a topic laid on your heart.

3. Discover the Big Idea

Each sermon has a theme. This is often called the big idea. It is the sermon in a nutshell. Compose a theme statement by writing it out. It should flow and have a ring to it that can be stated and restated throughout the sermon for those who hear to remember.

4. Determine Your Point of Structure

The key to outlining Biblical texts is to let the passage lead the process. If the text has four points, then the sermon will have four points. There is no correct number of sermon points. But, no sermon has to say everything the text says. Less is more when you want people to remember what you said, so keep that in mind. A sermon usually needs three sermon points to have enough length.

5. Explain Your Points

Declarative preaching seeks to convince listeners of the truth, but they won't be convinced of anything if they don't understand the points the preacher is making. Explanation of a point is an aid to understand. These supporting points are sometimes called subpoints.

6. Illustrate Your Points

If explanation aids in understanding a point, illustrations deepen it. Illustrations color in the idea, bringing depth to a discussion. It can be a true story of your own, someone else's story, a joke, skit, quotes, or object lessons. Here are a few websites to look up illustrations.

https://www.sermonillustrations.com
https://sermoncentral.com/sermon-illustrations
https://thepastorsworkshop.com
https://www.preachology.com/free-sermon-illustrations.html

7. Apply Your Points

Application pushes the listeners to action. Illustration says, "Let me describe what it looks like in real life." Generally, applications ought to be as concreate as possible. You want people to be doers of the Word.

8. Develop Your Introduction

The introduction of a declarative sermon exists to focus attention on and stimulate interest in the subject at hand. An introduction ought to be brief so as not to compete with the substance of the sermon. It should not be very long.

9. Create Your Conclusion

The points have been made. The stories have been told. Now is the time to close the deal, having brought the listeners to do what is required. The preacher should suggest specific, concrete action steps. An altar call can be appropriate here. The points can be restated for memory's sake!

10. Manage Your Transitions

The preacher needs to direct the flow of the sermon. This allows the listener to follow along easier.

We are going to look at Matthew 25:1-10 today. So, let's dive in…

First, next, third, last…

As we wrap it up, or in conclusion…

11. Title Your Sermon

Though preachers prefer to title their sermon at the beginning, it may be wise to wait until you complete the sermon. It needs to be creative to catch attention.

12. Prepare Your Notes

You need a skeleton to preach from! God can add to it or take away from it as you preach it, but a sermon outline is studying to show yourself approved, like Paul told Timothy.

Template for a Declarative Sermon

Title: _____

Good titles are creative and compelling, offering listeners a reason to listen, without giving too much away.

Theme (Big Idea): _____

Text: _____

State the main proposition in a complete and declarative statement of fewer than ten words with no ands.

I. Introduction

_____
_____
_____
_____
_____

Use an interesting story, an arresting quotation, or a useful statistic to gain the listener's attention.

II. Body

1. First Point: _____(Verse).

   A. Verse:

   _____
   _____
   _____
   _____

   B. Explanation:

   _____
   _____
   _____
   _____

   C. Illustration:

   _____
   _____
   _____
   _____

   D. Application:

   _____
   _____
   _____
   _____

2. Second Point: _____(Verse).

   A. Verse:

      _____

      _____

      _____

      _____

   B. Explanation:

      _____

      _____

      _____

      _____

   C. Illustration:

      _____

      _____

      _____

      _____

   D. Application:

      _____

      _____

      _____

      _____

3. Third Point: _____ (Verse).

    A. Verse:

       _____

       _____

       _____

       _____

    B. Explanation:

       _____

       _____

       _____

       _____

    C. Illustration:

       _____

       _____

       _____

       _____

    D. Application:

       _____

       _____

       _____

       _____

III. Conclusion

_____

_____

_____

_____

_____

The conclusion calls for a specific, measurable response from a listener in obedience to the message.

The Pragmatic Sermon:
Solve a Mystery

A pragmatic sermon is a type of sermon that focuses on the practical application of the teachings of the Word of God to the lives of the hearers. It is characterized by its ability to address the listener's needs and provide solutions to life's challenges. It is a need-oriented approach that seeks to apply the teachings of the Bible to real life situations.[6]

You are a detective! The steps to a pragmatic sermon are as follows[7]...

1. **Pray for Wisdom**

   The reality is, it is easy to misinterpret Scripture when you are focused only on a narrow application. So, pray for wisdom.

2. **Raise the Listener's Questions**

   What is it in the lives of your listeners that you are seeking to apply the Word to in this particular sermon? Let them know.

3. **List All the Possibilities**

   For instance, if the problem is one of marriage, your listener may be considering divorce. Is that the answer? There are many long-term results of this choice. Another choice might be to give up and just live in an unfulfilling marriage.

---

[6] https://www.preachingacts.com/how-to-make-a-pragmatic-sermon/

[7] Anderson, Kenton C, Choosing to Preach: A Comprehensive Introduction to Sermon Options and Structures: Grand Rapids. Michigan 49530 USA, Zondervan, 2006, page 161.

4. Eliminate the Illogical

Pragmatic preaching is cognitive preaching. It is inherently logical. So having lined up all the suspicious possibilities, we need to apply ruthless logic to them.

5. Gather all of Scripture's Wisdom

In this kind of message, you will likely use several Bible passages or verses. Use these to consider the evidence of God's inspired Word.

6. Answer the Listener's Question

Bring the answer to the forefront.

7. Apply the Insight Gained

Give examples of how the truth of Scripture makes a difference. Tell stories of people who have followed the wisdom of the Bible or give negative examples of those who didn't.

Sample of a Pragmatic Sermon

Myths that Make Us Miserable[8]
Text: Proverbs 4:23

The Listener's Question:

What can I do about the myths that can make me miserable?

I. Proposed Solutions:

1. It doesn't matter what you believe so long as you are sincere…Now, that sounds so good. It sounds so broad-minded, so tolerant…The only problem is it's absurd and irrational to hold this view. {Illustration: Following the wrong car.}

2. Don't believe everything you hear…A belief doesn't have to be true for it to affect you emotionally or cause emotional turmoil.

II. The Wisdom of Scripture (A Few of the Many Texts Offered)

1. John 8:32 – My guess is that we expose the lies that we've been taught by our culture and apply the truth.

2. Romans 3:4 – When it comes down to it, you have only two options. You have either the world or the Word of God. You will build your life on either what culture says or what Christ says. The world or the Word.

---

[8] A Sermon by Pastor Rick Warren of Saddleback Church in California

3. Luke 21:33 – God's Word has stood the test of time. You can trust it as your guidebook, as your authority, as your basis.

4. Matthew 7:24 – Do you want to get it together? You need to hear and you need to practice the truth.

5. Romans 12:2 – Would you like to be free from emotional hang-ups that keep you from being happy? It's possible. God can transform your mind and replace the old myths with a new system of beliefs based on the truth.

III. Answer the Question

1. The myths that make us miserable are destroyed by confrontation with the truth.

   A. Our beliefs have a fundamental, profound impact on our lives.
   B. False beliefs are often damaging.
   C. Truth is the key to overcoming the myths that make us miserable.

IV. Application

1. Commit to seeking the truth.

2. Commit to living the truth.

3. Commit to believing the truth.

CHAPTER 5

Delivery

We now move to the practical side of delivering a sermon. Delivery is a skill that is learned by time and some useful guidelines to consider. It is not to be confused with putting on a polished show to entertain others or get attention. It is more about moving personally out of the way to glorify Christ. Sermon delivery is about pointing to Jesus. Cutting down on distraction can help this.

The following is a sermon evaluation[9] form that can be used to improve communication when speaking on God's behalf. You are not disqualified as you work out these details and get better little by little.

Remember, the first time I spoke, I finished in 10 minutes on a Wednesday night at Westway Baptist Church. I read straight off my outline and did not look at a soul. I also sweat completely down. I did not give up and never preach again, though! It's a process, and every person is different. Be faithful to fulfill your call wherever and whatever your stage is in communicating. The time and effort will pay off.

---

[9] https://growchurch.net/sermon-evaluation-form-download

SERMON EVALUATION FORM

Preacher: _____ Date: _____

Evaluator: _____

Grade each section on a scale of 1 to 10, with 1 being poor and 10 being great.

CONTENT

1. Introduction: Was it engaging? Did it make you want to hear more? Did it introduce a problem we need a solution for?

- Poor 1 2 3 4 5 6 7 8 9 10 Great
- Comments:

2. Bible: Was scripture used and interpreted well as the foundation of the message?

- Poor 1 2 3 4 5 6 7 8 9 10 Great
- Comments:

3. Bottom Line: Can you summarize the main point of the sermon in a sentence?

- Poor 1 2 3 4 5 6 7 8 9 10 Great
- Comments:

4. Gospel: Was the good news of Jesus central to the message?

- Poor 1 2 3 4 5 6 7 8 9 10 Great
- Comments:

5. Clarity: Was anything said that was confusing, distracting, or too difficult to understand? Was there any Christian or insider language that was not explained for newcomers?

- Poor 1 2 3 4 5 6 7 8 9 10 Great
- Comments:

6. Application: Was there a clear call to action to apply the message to your life?
- Poor 1 2 3 4 5 6 7 8 9 10 Great
- Comments:

7. Illustrations: Were they used well? Did they connect with the audience? Did they help with the main point of the message?

- Poor 1 2 3 4 5 6 7 8 9 10 Great
- Comments:

8. Length: Was the sermon delivered within the given time? Were any parts too long or short?

- Poor 1 2 3 4 5 6 7 8 9 10 Great
- Comments:

9. Conclusion: Was the conclusion compelling? Did it summarize and drive the main point home? Did it end too fast or take too long?

- Poor 1 2 3 4 5 6 7 8 9 10 Great
- Comments:

10. Memorability: Were there any memorable phrases, illustrations, or application points that will help the message stick with people?

- Poor 1 2 3 4 5 6 7 8 9 10 Great
- Comments:

11. Objections: Did the preacher address any potential objections? Are there any objections that should have been addressed?

- Poor 1 2 3 4 5 6 7 8 9 10 Great
- Comments:

12. Unbelievers: Did the preacher speak to the people in the room who do not yet believe in Jesus?

- Poor 1 2 3 4 5 6 7 8 9 10 Great
- Comments:

DELIVERY

1. Gestures: Were gestures used appropriately to help communicate the message? Were any movements distracting (hands in pockets, fidgeting, playing with fingers, pacing, holding the pulpit)?

- Poor 1 2 3 4 5 6 7 8 9 10 Great
- Comments:

2. Pace: Did the preacher speak at an appropriate and varied pace? Was it too fast or slow? Were pauses used effectively?

- Poor 1 2 3 4 5 6 7 8 9 10 Great
- Comments:

3. Filler words: Did the preacher use any filler words repetitively (e.g., umm, like, ok, so, you know).

- Poor 1 2 3 4 5 6 7 8 9 10 Great
- Comments:

4. Authenticity: Did the preacher seem confident with the material? Were they too tied to their notes? Were they passionate? Did they appear to truly believe what they said?

- Poor 1 2 3 4 5 6 7 8 9 10 Great
- Comments:

5. Engagement: Did the sermon keep your interest? Were any parts boring or irrelevant? Did the audience respond (laugh, cry, clap, raise hands, "Amen," cheer).

- Poor 1 2 3 4 5 6 7 8 9 10 Great
- Comments:

6. Tech: Were there any problems with the microphone, sound, lighting, videos, or slides used?

- Poor 1 2 3 4 5 6 7 8 9 10 Great
- Comments:

7. Nervous: Did the speaker say they were nervous to those they were speaking to one or more times?

- Poor 1 2 3 4 5 6 7 8 9 10 Great
- Comments:

8. Dress: Was there anything distracting or sloppy about the speaker's dress or appearance? Did it fit the audience they were speaking too?

- Poor 1 2 3 4 5 6 7 8 9 10 Great
- Comments:

CHAPTER 6

What Covenant Will You Preach?

One of the things I have tried to do over the years is to cut down on my sugar intake. In an effort to accomplish this, I have used sugar free chocolate pudding to make chocolate milk. I love chocolate milk! It makes me want to drink some while typing this sentence! There is something interesting about using sugar free chocolate pudding to make chocolate milk, it does not mix as well as regular chocolate powder. It partially mixes. Clumps that do not bond with the milk after stirring float back to the top and stick to the side of the glass.

Jesus was clear, the Old Covenant and the New Covenant do **NOT** mix.

"No one sews a patch of unshrunk cloth on an old garment, for the patch will pull away from the garment, making the tear worse. Neither do people pour new wine into old wineskins. If they do, the skins will burst; the wine will run out and the wineskins will be ruined. No, they pour new wine into new wineskins, and both are preserved." (Matthew 9:16-17)

The new wine is the New Covenant, and the old wineskin is the Old Covenant. The patch of unshrunk cloth is the New Covenant, and the old garment is the Old Covenant.

1. How did Jesus discourage mixing the covenants?

   _____

   _____

   _____

   _____

   _____

Jesus gave an important command for us preachers... and teachers...

"Then Jesus came to them and said, 'All authority in heaven and on earth has been given to me. Therefore go and make disciples of all nations, baptizing them in the name of the Father and of the Son and of the Holy Spirit, and teaching them to obey everything I have commanded you. And surely I am with you always, to the very end of the age.'" (Matthew 28:18-20)

This is called the Great Commission.

2.   What did Jesus say to do?

_____
_____
_____
_____
_____

    Jesus fulfilled the Old Covenant and taught the New Covenant that He established. So, Jesus told us preachers and teachers to teach others to obey what He commanded. It was a command to teach the <u>NEW COVENANT</u>.

    I have learned over the years that the best way to not mix the covenants as Jesus desired is to first, ask a question. "What covenant is this?" Know where you are in the Bible. Many think the New Covenant began when you get to the page between Malachi and Matthew that says New Testament. God did not put that there, man did. When did the New Covenant start?

    Let's find out!...

*"On the first day of the Festival of Unleavened Bread, the disciples came to Jesus and asked, "Where do you want us to make preparations for you to eat the Passover?" He replied, "Go into the city to a certain man and tell him, 'The Teacher says: My appointed time is near. I am going to celebrate the Passover with my disciples at your house.'" So the disciples did as Jesus had directed them and prepared the Passover. When evening came, Jesus was reclining at the table with the Twelve. And while they were eating, he said, "Truly I tell you, one of you will betray me." They were very sad and began to say to him one after the other, "Surely you don't mean me, Lord?" Jesus replied, "The one who has dipped his hand into the bowl with me will betray me. The Son of Man will go just as it is written about him. But woe to that man who betrays the Son of Man! It would be better for him if he had not been born." Then Judas, the one who would betray him, said, "Surely you don't mean me, Rabbi?" Jesus answered, "You have said so." **While they were eating, Jesus took bread, and when he had given thanks, he broke it and gave it to his disciples, saying, "Take and eat; this is my body." Then he took a cup, and when he had given thanks, he gave it to them, saying, "Drink from it, all of you. This is my blood of the covenant, which is poured out for many for the forgiveness of sins.** I tell you, I will not drink from this fruit of the vine from now on until that day when I drink it new with you in my Father's kingdom." When they had sung a hymn, they went out to the Mount of Olives."* (Matthew 26:17-30)

3. When did the New Covenant start according to Jesus (Matthew 26:26-28)?

_____

_____

_____

_____

_____

The New Covenant began at Jesus' death and resurrection. That means everything in the Bible after that is the New Covenant. The things Jesus said and did before His death were spoken and done under the Old Covenant and fulfilling it. The sermon on the mount was to show those who thought they were good enough to get into heaven they were sinners in need of a Savior and could not do it themselves. The law only shows sin and cannot save.

The Old Covenant is used by the disciples in the Bible after Jesus death, but it was used to support the New Covenant and used properly. Those who mixed the Old Covenant and the New Covenant were upset with the Apostle Paul and opposed grace by adding Jesus plus something to be saved. Paul called them Judaizers and opposed them vehemently. He later spoke about those who misused the Old Covenant and tried to mix it with Christianity.

"The goal of this command is love, which comes from a pure heart and a good conscience and a sincere faith. Some have departed from these and have turned to meaningless talk. They want to be teachers of the law, but they do not know what they are talking about or what they so confidently affirm. We know that the law is good if one uses it properly. We also know that the law is made not for the righteous but for lawbreakers and rebels, the ungodly and sinful, the unholy and irreligious, for those who kill their fathers or mothers, for murderers, for the sexually immoral, for those practicing homosexuality, for slave traders and liars and perjurers—and for whatever else is contrary to the sound doctrine that conforms to the gospel concerning the glory of the blessed God, which he entrusted to me." (1 Timothy 1:5-11)

4. How did the Apostle describe those mixing the covenants (1 Timothy 1:5-7)?

_____

_____

_____

_____

_____

5. The law is good if one uses it in what way (1 Timothy 1:8)?

_____

_____

_____

_____

_____

6. Who is the law for instead of the saved (1 Timothy 1:9-11)?

_____

_____

_____

_____

_____

The Old Covenant was fulfilled by Jesus and He replaced it with the New Covenant.

CHAPTER 7

Sermon Samples

The following are examples of sermons I have preached in the past and I hope they will help you create your own sermons.

Fleshing Out the Golden Rule

4/6/2025

I.   Introduction

1. In May, at the end of her freshman year at the University of Tampa, Kira Rumfola packed her bags and headed to the airport with her favorite roommate: a colorful betta fish named Theo. Rumfola, 19, was headed home to Long Island for the summer and was happy to be bringing home the little fish she had bonded with during the months she'd had him. She figured there would be no problem taking Theo aboard the plane in a small portable fish carrier.

    A. "I'd done it before over the holidays with another airline, so I filled the container with water and put Theo in it," she said. But there was a problem. While she was checking her bags for her flight on Southwest Airlines, customer service agent Ismael Lazo noticed the deep blue and purple fish and explained to Rumfola that the airline's pet policy allowed only small dogs and cats on board in carriers. No other pets are permitted on planes. "All of my roommates had already gone home for the summer and I had nobody to leave Theo with," said Rumfola, who is majoring in early-childhood education at the university. "I was really sad and wondered what I was going to do," she said. "He's my pet."

    B. Lazo, 35, said he understood Rumfola's concern for Theo. "I have two dogs - I wouldn't want to abandon them somewhere," he said. "And I also know how hard it is to leave them when I go out of town." So, he made a split-second decision to offer his home and his fish-sitting services. "How about if I take your fish home to live with me and my fiancée until you come back for college in the fall?" he told her. "You can text me over the summer to see how he's doing whenever you like."

2. I am not sure if Lazo, who worked for Southwest Airlines, knew the golden rule, but he sure practiced it.

3. The golden rule is found in Luke 6:31, *"Do to others as you would have them do to you."*

    A. It is stated in a different way in Matthew 7:12, *"So in everything, do to others what you would have them do to you, for this sums up the Law and the Prophets."*

4. I think we would all agree that it is easy to practice the golden rule when someone hasn't gotten on our nerves, but harder when there is a problem at hand. Does being at personal odds with someone excuse us from following the golden rule? Let the Bible answer this question itself.

    A. *"If you love those who love you, what credit is that to you? Even sinners love those who love them. And if you do good to those who are good to you, what credit is that to you? Even sinners do that. And if you lend to those from whom you expect repayment, what credit is that to you? Even sinners lend to sinners, expecting to be repaid in full. But love your enemies, do good to them, and lend to them without expecting to get anything back. Then your reward will be great, and you will be children of the Most High, because he is kind to the ungrateful and wicked. Be merciful, just as your Father is merciful." (Luke 6:32-36)*

1.) Jesus establishes a higher standard for those of us who bear the name Christian.

    A.) Unbelievers are good to those who are good to them. That is the norm.

    B.) Believers are to be good to those who are not good to them. This is what is rewarded by God.

5. Now, we are going to look at four ways to live out the golden rule when it is not so easy to do so.

II. Body

1. Follow the golden rule by expressing your feelings instead of criticizing (Proverbs 15:1; Philippians 4:2-3; James 1:19-20).

    A. It is only a matter of time when someone will rub you the wrong way. At those moments, there will be a choice to follow the Holy Spirit or act out in the flesh.

    B. Proverbs 15:1 says, *"A gentle answer turns away wrath, but a harsh word stirs up anger."*

    C. Walking in the Holy Spirit will lead to giving a gentle answer, but if you speak harshly your flesh will be on full display.

        1.) Gentle means tender, faint-hearted, soft, and weak.

            A.) Being gentle is to appear weak, but it really shows strength to be tender, faint-hearted, and soft in response.

2.) Harsh means painful, pang, grievous, and sorrow.

D. Good people can get crossways and do not have to let it go sideways.
    1.) Philippians 4:2-3 says, *"I plead with Euodia and I plead with Syntyche to be of the same mind in the Lord. Yes, and I ask you, my true companion, help these women since they have contended at my side in the cause of the gospel, along with Clement and the rest of my co-workers, whose names are in the book of life."*

        A.) Euodia and Syntyche had been harsh with one another. Gentleness had been thrown out the door! Paul asked for these two women to be of the same mind and remember they are both going to Heaven.

E. Let's be real that it feels good to criticize when we have been offended or hurt. It is not showing the golden rule, though. Would you rather be criticized or receive a gentle answer during disagreement?

F. One way you can give a gentle answer is to take the attack out of what needs to be said and leave room that you could be wrong. This can be done by using "I" statements. "I felt disappointed when you showed up late." Vs. "You are a loser because you were late and a big disappointment." See the difference? One is gentle and one is harsh.

G. *"My dear brothers and sisters, take note of this: Everyone should be quick to listen, slow to speak and slow to become angry, because human anger does not produce the righteousness that God desires." (James 1:19-20)*

2. Follow the golden rule by appreciating instead of showing contempt (1 Corinthians 1:4-9; Genesis 1:7-8; Matthew 5:21-22; 1 Thessalonians 5:11).

   A. The Apostle Paul did this despite the Corinthian Church having so many problems. Listen to what he said before he addressed the divisiveness.

   B. *"I always thank my God for you because of his grace given you in Christ Jesus. For in him you have been enriched in every way— with all kinds of speech and with all knowledge— God thus confirming our testimony about Christ among you. Therefore you do not lack any spiritual gift as you eagerly wait for our Lord Jesus Christ to be revealed. He will also keep you firm to the end, so that you will be blameless on the day of our Lord Jesus Christ. God is faithful, who has called you into fellowship with his Son, Jesus Christ our Lord." (1 Corinthians 1:4-9)*

   C. Contempt is defined as the act of despising: the state of mind of one who despises and a lack of respect or reverence for something.

   D. When we have a disagreement with someone and show them contempt, a line is crossed.

      1.) Contempt is attacking the self-worth of another person with an intent to insult or abuse.

      2.) The Golden Rule says, "You would not want to be on the receiving end of contempt destroying your self-worth. Then why would you do it someone else?"

   E. We would do well to remember these verses when it comes to the self-worth of those we have an issue with at times.

1.) The person you want to show contempt towards is made in God's image. *"So God created mankind in his own image, in the image of God he created them; male and female he created them."* *(Genesis 1:7-8)* Something made in God's image has immerse value. Who are we to devalue what God has already valued?

2.) The attack of another person's self-worth is dangerous. *"You have heard that it was said to the people long ago, 'You shall not murder, and anyone who murders will be subject to judgment.' But I tell you that anyone who is angry with a brother or sister will be subject to judgment. Again, anyone who says to a brother or sister, 'Raca,' is answerable to the court. And anyone who says, 'You fool!' will be in danger of the fire of hell."* *(Matthew 5:21-22)* Showing contempt is always done in anger, and in what Jesus said, it was telling someone else "Raca" or "You Fool." How can that be compared to murder? You are murdering their self-worth. Raca means empty headed person. Fool means dull, stupid, shut up, blockhead, and absurd.

F. To live the golden rule instead of showing contempt is to show appreciation. Build a culture of appreciation.

1.) Remind yourself of the person's positive qualities or find something to be grateful for about them.

2.) *"Therefore encourage one another and build each other up, just as in fact you are doing."* *(1 Thessalonians 5:11)* This helps you too, as what you think becomes what you feel, and what you feel becomes what you do.

3. Follow the golden rule by taking responsibility instead of blaming others (Genesis 3:11-13; James 5:16; 1 Samuel 13:7-12).

A. We can see this from the beginning of the Bible.

B. To Adam, God said, *"And he said, "Who told you that you were naked? Have you eaten from the tree that I commanded you not to eat from?" (Genesis 3:11)*

    1.) Adam took responsibility and said, "I sinned and ate of the tree."

    2.) Nope, *"The man said, "The woman you put here with me—she gave me some fruit from the tree, and I ate it."*

    3.) He dodges responsibility and blames Eve.

C. To Eve, God said, *"Then the Lord God said to the woman, "What is this you have done? ..." (Genesis 3:13a)*
    1.) Eve took responsibility and said, "I sinned and ate of the tree."

    2.) Nope, *"The woman said, "The serpent deceived me, and I ate."* *(Genesis 3:13b)*

    3.) She dodges responsibility and blames the devil.

D. Not taking responsibility for your part is a form of defensiveness. It reverses the blame.

E. Taking responsibility is accepting the perspective of the other person and offering an apology for wrongdoing.

F. Apologizing is practicing the golden rule.
   "Therefore confess your sins to each other and pray for each other so that you may be healed. The prayer of a righteous person is powerful and effective." (James 5:16)

G. The lack of doing so can be seen in the relationship between King Saul and the Prophet Samuel.
   "Some Hebrews even crossed the Jordan to the land of Gad and Gilead. Saul remained at Gilgal, and all the troops with him were quaking with fear. He waited seven days, the time set by Samuel; but Samuel did not come to Gilgal, and Saul's men began to scatter. So he said, "Bring me the burnt offering and the fellowship offerings." And Saul offered up the burnt offering. Just as he finished making the offering, Samuel arrived, and Saul went out to greet him. "What have you done?" asked Samuel. Saul replied, "When I saw that the men were scattering, and that you did not come at the set time, and that the Philistines were assembling at Mikmash, I thought, 'Now the Philistines will come down against me at Gilgal, and I have not sought the Lord's favor.' So I felt compelled to offer the burnt offering." (1 Samuel 13:7-12)

H. King Saul said, "I know I was wrong in not waiting and making the offering." Nope. He blamed the prophet Samuel for not showing up on time.

I. The rule is practiced when we listen to the perspective of the other (Samuel) and offer an apology for any wrongdoing (Saul).

III. Conclusion

1. Today, we learned that it is easy to practice the golden rule if things are going well between us and others, but harder when there is a problem at hand.

2. In those times…

    A. Give a gentle answer instead of a harsh one. It can be done by "I feel" statements and leaving room for being wrong yourself.

    B. Give appreciation instead of showing contempt by finding something about the person to give thanks for.

    C. Give the gift of an apology instead of shifting blame to someone else though you might not be the one totally at fault.

Good and Evil

Part 1

I.   Introduction

1. The headlines on September 4th read, two 14-year-old students and two teachers were killed in a mass shooting at Apalachee High School in Winder, Georgia. Nine other people — eight students and one teacher — were wounded and hospitalized, all of whom are expected to survive. That is evil.

    A. The question of good and evil is one of the number one questions that many people have about God.

    1.) Why do bad things happen to good people?
    2.) How could God allow this?

    B. George Barna, a Christian public pollster, did a national survey in which he asked, "If you could ask God only one question and you knew He would answer, what would you ask?" The top response was, "Why is there pain and suffering in the world?"

2. It is good to ask these types of questions of God. A quick reading through the book of Psalms shows that David asked deep and searching questions to God. He was unafraid to ask almost anything, and he was called a man after God's own heart. His questions led to faith filled answers as ours should.

3. One of the ways that people try to deal with the problem of evil is through DENIAL. This happens in four ways we try to figure it out on our own.

    A. Deny GOD exists.

    B. Deny God is GREAT, as it seems, sometimes, He does not have the power to help with the problem of evil.

C. Deny God is GOOD.

D. Deny EVIL exists. It is just an illusion, or God would never allow me to experience evil.

4. Any form of these denials does not provide answers to the problem of evil. They only leave us disappointed and hopeless.

A. Why does evil exist in the world? Let's look to the Bible for answers as it does provide concrete hope.

II.   Why does evil exist in God's world? THREE TRUTHS

1. God is GOOD (Psalm 100:5, Genesis 1:31).

A. The starting place of any discussion of evil in the world must be these three words: God is good. There is just too much good in this world to deny the goodness of the Creator. He is the source of all the good in the world. There is only good because of Him. Why do we look for the bad in the world and fixate on it instead of looking for the good in the world and fixate on it? Do we love bad news?

B. His CHARACTER is good (Psalms 100:5).

1.) *"For the Lord is good and his love endures forever; his faithfulness continues through all generations." (Psalms 10:5)*

2.) He is always good when evil happens to us or others. His love endures forever during evil times. He is always faithful amid chaos. We can count on His character that is unchanging.

C. His ACTIONS are good (Genesis 1:31).

1.) *"God saw all that he had made, and it was very good. And there was evening, and there was morning—the sixth day." (Genesis 1:31)*

2.) God only speaks good things and does good things. No exceptions. God does no evil. Don't blame Him. He started everything as we know it and said it is good, and about humans, very good. There is only good in the world because He is good.

2. God is ALL-POWERFUL (Jeremiah 32:18b).

   A. *"...Great and mighty God, whose name is the Lord Almighty."* *(Jeremiah 32:18b)*

   B. All-powerful means exactly what it says. God has the power to do anything. However, and this is important, He does not do what violates His goodness or character.

   C. Since God is all-powerful and can do anything, that means when He chooses to not stop evil at a given moment, He has a reason. I don't like this answer, but it is true.

   D. I remember the death that really impacted me as a kid. My grandma Mabel got sick. I prayed she would be healed. She passed and went to be with the Lord. She is the one who made me promise to memorize Psalms 23. He could have healed her, but He didn't. I had to accept this. The next point is the one that throws us for a loop.

3. The WORLD is evil (John 3:19, 1 John 2:15).

   A. The Bible tells us the world is evil.

   B. *"This is the verdict: Light has come into the world, but people loved darkness instead of light because their deeds were evil."* *(John 3:19)*

      1.) There is good in this world! Jesus is the light and His light vanquishes the foe of darkness. The problem is that people love the darkness and want to do evil.

C. *"Do not love the world or anything in the world. If anyone loves the world, love for the Father is not in them." (1 John 2:15)*

    1.) The expectations of those of us who are Christians is not to love the evil in the world. We are to love the Lord instead with all our heart, soul, mind, and body.

    2.) Love, in this passage, means being a friend of evil. Who wants an evil friend? Likewise, why would you befriend evil by accepting, promoting, or participating in it?

    3.) World, in this passage, means the things in the world that are opposed to God and the things He calls evil. We can't call evil things good and good things evil. We must call good, good and evil, evil. We currently live in world that calls sinful actions good and those who oppose the sin as evil. It's backward (perverse).

III.   How can all of these be true?

- Since God is good, how can evil exist? Since He is all-powerful, why doesn't He stop all evil? How can He allow good and evil to exist at the same time in the world? It can be summed up on one simple reason…

1. There is no love without CHOICE.

    A. God could have made a person who never could have chosen to sin, but that person would have been denied the opportunity to love.

    B. The choice God gave us was to say YES to a relationship with Him. This also means we can say NO to Him and all kinds of evil happen in the world as a result.

    C. Choice gives us the opportunity to do the WRONG thing, to not LOVE Him. To not love God is the ultimate EVIL. That ultimate evil results in all the evil we see in the world.

2. Two Truths to Remember

A. God is SOVEREIGN.

B. Mankind has a FREE choice.

1.) How do we reconcile these two? God gives us choice, doesn't that put us in control rather than Him? Our God is an awesome God! He is able to give us, as part of His creation, a free will to decide and yet remain in complete control of creation. How does He do that? He is God.

2.) Be sure to keep these truths in balance. If you lean too far into God being in full control, you come down on the side of fatalism. It doesn't matter what you do. That is not true. If you lean too far toward man's free will, you come down on the side of humanism that we are in control of our fate. That is not true. The answer is in the middle.

IV. Why does God continue to allow evil instead of stopping it?

- This is a question that we struggle with. We need to remember a couple of things.

1. He already has DEFEATED evil (1 Corinthians 15:57, Colossians 2:15).

A. *"But thanks be to God! He gives us the victory through our Lord Jesus Christ." (1 Corinthians 15:57)*

B. *"And having disarmed the powers and authorities, he made a public spectacle of them, triumphing over them by the cross." (Colossians 2:15)*

C. He defeated evil at the cross and will allow us to join Him in the victory for all eternity. We are currently fighting a battle in which the ultimate victory is assured.

D. This gives us hope as we fight. We have read the end of the book. One day we will join Him, victorious in Heaven.

E. Why does God wait for that day? Why doesn't He end evil now?

2. He is PATIENT (1 John 2:2, 1 Timothy 2:3-4, 2 Peter 3:9).

    A. Evil in this world can break our heart and make us cry in pain. How do you think it makes God feel?

    B. If it hurts your heart, what does it do to His heart? His heart cries more than ours. He hurts over sin and the problem of evil more than we can possibly imagine.

        1.) God has provided for the salvation of all if they want it (1 John 2:2).

            A.) *"He is the atoning sacrifice for our sins, and not only for ours but also for the sins of the whole world." (1 John 2:2)*

        2.) God desires for all to be saved (1 Timothy 2:3-4).

            A.) *"This is good, and pleases God our Savior, who wants all people to be saved and to come to a knowledge of the truth." (1 Timothy 2:3-4)* He did His part! We must do ours. No one has to go to hell, but it is a reality people choose.

        3.) And He WAITS patiently (2 Peter 3:9).

            A.) *"The Lord is not slow in keeping his promise, as some understand slowness. Instead, he is patient with you, not wanting anyone to perish, but everyone to come to repentance." (2 Peter 3:9)*

            B.) Why hasn't the rapture happened? He wants more saved before it!

C.) Why hasn't He stopped evil totally? He wants more saved, and then the Second Coming at the end of the seven years will occur, stopping people from doing evil.

V. Conclusion

1. In the end, the only solution to the problem of evil is trust. How much do you trust God?

   A. When you trust God, you're not afraid to ask the tough questions and His answers give the needed assurance.

   B. When you trust God, you're not afraid to admit that much of the evil in our lives is our own doing – trust releases you from your need to blame.

   C. When you trust God, you begin to get a glimpse of things in the light of eternity. People are not getting away with evil.

   D. When you trust God, you feel His compassion for us as we face evil in the world.

   E. When you trust God, you may or may not get your answer for the question you have, but even without the answer, you can trust the answerer.

Check out other books written by Charles Thompson that may encourage your faith.

Are you ready to live with eternity in mind?

"Answer the Call" invites you on a transformative journey through the book of 1 Timothy, designed to deepen your faith, sharpen your discernment, and empower you to walk confidently in your God-given calling. This comprehensive guide offers practical insights for spiritual growth, bold use of your gifts, and bridging generational gaps within the Church.

Explore essential topics such as leading with compassion, honoring widows, managing finances wisely, and living a purpose-driven life. Discover how to understand Old Testament laws, embrace the depth of God's forgiveness, and protect your heart against false teachings.

Learn to cultivate a personal prayer life, dress in a way that honors the Lord, and recognize or become a godly leader. This book encourages you to grow spiritually while operating in your unique gifts, connect meaningfully across generations, and serve others selflessly.

With each page, you'll find inspiration to live every day with eternity in mind. Delve into the wisdom and grace that will guide you to honor God, lead with integrity, and impact the lives of others for His glory.

Join this journey and let your perspective on eternity shape everything you do.

Have obsessions and compulsions paralyzed your life? Does it seem like your battle with obsessive compulsive disorder is leading you in circles with no way out?

You can learn from the Israelites in the Old Testament who were fearful to enter the promised land and two men who were different. Joshua and Caleb stood out in the crowd due to the faith they exhibited. Both inherited what God had promised.

By having faith, you can walk in their footsteps and inherit your promised land—one in which OCD does not rule your life.

Charles Thompson, who suffers from OCD himself, provides tools to boost your faith through prayer, Bible study, spiritual warfare, and devotionals while incorporating established medical methods.

The workbook will help you confront OCD by looking at it through God's eyes. You'll find that anxiety and pressure can be relieved—and that God has a loving plan for you. This is the first Christian workbook on the subject!

Check out Pastor Charles' Amazon author page for these and other available titles!

CERTIFICATE

OF ACHIEVEMENT

This Certifies that

Has successfully completed

BIBLICAL PREACHING 101

WORKBOOK: From Calling to Confidence

Charles Thompson

Pastor/Author/Teacher

Date

www.ingramcontent.com/pod-product-compliance
Lightning Source LLC
Chambersburg PA
CBHW041118120626
46547CB00019B/2761